Taís Rodrigues Dib
Débora Maniglia

The inclusion of people with disabilities in public schools

Taís Rodrigues Dib
Débora Maniglia

The inclusion of people with disabilities in public schools

The educators' perspective

ScienciaScripts

Imprint

Cover image: www.ingimage.com

This book is a translation from the original published under ISBN 978-3-330-76028-8.

Publisher:
Sciencia Scripts
is a trademark of
Dodo Books Indian Ocean Ltd. and OmniScriptum S.R.L publishing group

120 High Road, East Finchley, London, N2 9ED, United Kingdom
Str. Armeneasca 28/1, office 1, Chisinau MD-2012, Republic of Moldova, Europe
Printed at: see last page
ISBN: 978-620-8-07914-7

We dedicate it to the professionals who work in inclusive education and especially to all people with disabilities.

"It's important to start from the principle that everyone at school, regardless of their job or disability, benefits students, teachers and society in general. Children's contact with each other reinforces positive attitudes, helping them to learn to be sensitive, to understand, to respect and to grow, living with the individual differences and similarities between their peers. All children, without distinction, can benefit from the experiences gained in the educational environment. Students with disabilities, in particular, can perform better educationally, socially and occupationally when in inclusive environments. They learn how to act and interact with their peers in the "real" world, and the greatest benefit for teachers is co-participation in the transformation of the school, through cooperative support and the enhancement of professional skills. The advantages and benefits of this integration work can be seen in the enrichment and development of the school environment and all those who are part of it. "

(FERREIRA, 2003)

INDICE

INTRODUCTION

Based on current discussions around the issue of the educational inclusion of people with disabilities, this research focuses on understanding this process, taking the municipality of Franca/SP as its focus. To this end, the research was carried out in a municipal primary school, with the aim of analyzing the issue from the perspective of the professionals involved in this context, highlighting the importance of the inclusion of a Social Work professional in this process.

Faced with this mobilization for the inclusion of students with special needs in the regular school system, the school has taken on a challenging role in guaranteeing that everyone has access to and remains in school, a right guaranteed by law, with the ultimate aim of providing a quality education that enables them to live an independent life and take a critical look at the reality in which they live. This is why we became interested in the topic **"The process of inclusion of people with disabilities in the municipal school system of Franca/SP: the perspective of educators",** in order to understand how this process is taking place, because in order for the school to adapt to this new school model, it is important to restructure so that all students can live together in a suitable environment, as well as reorganizing the pedagogical proposal on offer.

For a better conception of the inclusive process, an updated bibliographic study was carried out with publications related to this theme, its legislation and the importance of a social service professional in the educational area, characterizing a bibliographic research.

The work was guided by a qualitative perspective, based on historical-dialectical materialism, because qualitative research allows us to analyze the depth of situations and get closer to the research subjects. According to Alves

(1991), "Reality is a social construction in which the researcher participates", thus making it possible to understand phenomena from a historical perspective and interpret the interrelationships of a given context, allowing the researcher and the researched to be in a broad process of interaction.

The subjects of this research were: a pedagogical coordinator; a pedagogue and three elementary school teachers working at the "Escola Municipal de Educapao Basica Professora Sueli Contini Marques", who had students with disabilities in their classrooms. First of all, we contacted the principal of the school to present our proposal, and she was very supportive of the work, so we already scheduled the interviews.

We carried out semi-structured interviews, with basic questions based on the theme of the research, which allowed us to create new hypotheses based on the informants' answers (TRIVINOS, 1987), and thus ensure greater reflection and debate in relation to special education. Still according to Trivinos (1987), the purpose of the questions is to determine the immediate and immediate reasons for the social phenomenon, and they can be called explanatory or causal, from a historical-dialectical perspective.

The interviews were therefore carried out at the school, and the professionals involved showed great interest in the subject. They were initially recorded on a tape recorder, with the permission of the research subjects, and then transcribed for data collection and analysis. The script can be found in the appendix. The results were interpreted using the content analysis described by Bardin (1977). According to this author, content analysis is a set of techniques that make it possible to achieve indicators that allow us to obtain knowledge relating to the subject studied, ensuring the objectivity, systematization and influence of the interviewees' statements.

> It is currently used to study and analyze qualitative material, seeking a better understanding of a communication or discourse, delving into its grammatical, ideological and other characteristics, as well as extracting the most relevant aspects (BARDIN, 1977).

As a complement to this analysis, the research was approached from the perspective of totality, in order to understand the universality, particularity and singularity present in the reality of the school, being able to reach the essence of the phenomenon and contribute to the destruction of pseudo-concreticity, as Karel Kosic (1976) assures.

In order to analyze the inclusion that has taken place at the school, in the first chapter: **"Inclusive education for people with disabilities"**, we discuss the concept of disability and existing legislation, which clarifies the obligation for schools to welcome and enroll all students, regardless of their particularities. Considering that this inclusion alone is insufficient, the education system must cater for everyone according to their needs, so that they remain in school with a quality education that guarantees learning and the development of their potential. With this in mind, we analyzed the frequency of students with disabilities in regular schools in Brazil and in the state of Sao Paulo, using statistical data provided by government agencies.

In the second chapter **"The necessary conditions for the operationalization of inclusive education for people with disabilities"**, we emphasized the training of educators, stressing that, for the success of this inclusion process, school management and especially the participation of the teacher is essential, as they are directly linked to the therefore, we believe it is important to understand the role of the school and the role of the teacher in this process.

And finally, in the third chapter **"The inclusion of students with disabilities in regular municipal education in Franca/SP"**, we analyzed education in the municipality of Franca and interpreted the interviews conducted with education professionals, who represent the understanding of this process in this part of reality. Although there are no social workers working on the issue of inclusion in the field of education in this municipality, we consider it important to analyze the understanding that educators have of the role of this professional in this socio-occupational space, so we highlight the contribution of the social worker in this context.

In the light of this approach, we were able to understand that inclusion from the point of view of education professionals is still not really happening. The school doesn't have all the resources it needs to help educate students with special educational needs, and most of the time the responsibility for the success of this process lies with the individual efforts of the teachers. In this context, we find a number of possible contributions from social work professionals from the school's perspective, focusing on the challenge of ensuring that inclusion is achieved, with quality education, success in learning and the all-round development of individuals with special educational needs.

CHAPTER I INCLUSIVE EDUCATION FOR PEOPLE WITH DISABILITIES

In this chapter, we will investigate the historical context of people with disabilities, from the time they were excluded and abandoned by society, through the specific care provided to the proposal to include them in ordinary education. For a better understanding of this process, we will detail the legislation on education that has been achieved for this category, in order to better understand the origin of inclusion and the whole process that guarantees access for people with disabilities to the Brazilian education system.

Before we present public policies in the field of special education, let's start by defining what disability is.

1.1 Concept of Disability

Disability is any type of impairment that causes difficulties, incapacities or impossibilities in the performance of activities that are common in the daily lives of people considered "normal", such as the simple act of getting around, communicating, receiving or transmitting information, giving oneself socially, understanding facts and/or the reality in which one lives, as well as motor coordination and spatial orientation (Decree No. 3.298).

There are different types of disability: physical, mental/intellectual, visual, hearing and multiple. According to Decree No. 5.296[1] of 2004, Physical Disability is when physical function is impaired through a complete or partial

[1] Regulates Laws n°s 10.048, of November 8, 2000, which gives priority service to the people it specifies, and 10.098, of December 19, 2000, which establishes general rules and basic criteria for promoting accessibility for people with disabilities or reduced mobility, and makes other provisions (BRASIL, 2004, online).

alteration of one or more segments of the human body,

> [...] presenting as paraplegia, paraparesis, monoplegia, monoparesis, tetraplegia, tetraparesis, triplegia, triparesis, hemiplegia, hemiparesis, ostomy, amputation or absence of limb, cerebral palsy, dwarfism, limbs with congenital or acquired deformity, except aesthetic deformities and those that do not produce difficulties for the performance of functions (BRASIL, 2004, online).

Mental/intellectual disability manifests itself before the age of eighteen when the intellectual capacity is below average, in addition to having

> [...] limitations associated with two or more areas of adaptive skills, such as: communication, personal care, social skills, use of community resources, health and safety, academic skills, leisure and work (BRASIL, 2004, online).

Visual impairment can occur through

> [...] blindness, in which visual acuity is equal to or less than 0.05 in the better eye, with the best optical correction; low vision, which means visual acuity between 0.3 and 0.05 in the better eye, with the best optical correction; cases in which the sum of the visual field measurement in both eyes is equal to or less than 60o; or the simultaneous occurrence of any of the previous conditions (BRASIL, 2004, online).

Hearing impairment is the "bilateral loss, partial or total, of forty-one decibels (dB) or more, measured by audiogram at frequencies of 500Hz, 1,000Hz, 2,000Hz and 3,000Hz" (BRASIL, 2004, online).

Multiple Disabilities are characterized by the combination of two or more associated physical, sensory, mental, emotional or social behavioral impairments, not only the sum of these, but also the combination of two or more physical, sensory, mental, emotional or social impairments.

level of development and communication and learning skills.

There are specific terminologies for this area, the most recent and most appropriate being "People with Disabilities", suggested by Sassaki (2006), who is a consultant in the area of Social Inclusion, but the term "People with Disabilities (PWD)" is still used in state and federal documentation. Other terms also used are: "People with Special Needs (PNE)" and "People with Special Educational Needs", however these nomenclatures are not suitable to be used to identify people with disabilities, as not all people with special needs are necessarily disabled and not all people with disabilities need special educational resources.

The author Diniz (2007) criticizes the concept of disability as a biological disadvantage, recognizing the injured body, but associating society's oppression with governmental neglect, i.e. if there were support and accessibility networks that guarantee a diversity of lifestyles, the integration of the disabled would actually occur.

1.2 A Brief History of Special Education in Brazil

In order to analyze the evolution of inclusive education, it is important to consider the different historical and cultural phases of the process of social inclusion of people with disabilities, and for this we will cite two of the main authors who discuss the subject: Mazzotta (2005) and Sassaki (2006).

According to Mazzotta (2005), it is possible to highlight three stages that portray social customs in this context. First, marginalization, a phase of total disbelief and abandonment of these individuals, during which time society did not organize itself in the search for services for this segment. Then there was the welfare phase, which provided protection for people with disabilities based on philanthropy, humanitarianism and paternalism, during which time there was still no belief in the potential of these individuals. Finally, the education/rehabilitation phase, which was marked by educational organizations and services based on a belief in the potential and development of people with disabilities.

When analyzing this process of educational inclusion, Sassaki (2006) divides it into four phases:

- Exclusion phase - people with disabilities were ignored by society;
- Phase of institutional segregation - these individuals received care in philanthropic or religious institutions, and were excluded from social life, including their families. It is important to note that special schools and rehabilitation centers appeared during this period;
- The integration phase saw the start of regular schools, special classes[2] and resource rooms[3] so that people with special needs could get used to society;
- Inclusion phase - the period during which people with disabilities are included in the mainstream education system, adapting classrooms and teaching processes to cater for students according to their specific needs.

At the end of the 18th century and the beginning of the 19th century, specialized institutionalization, accompanied by the rapid expansion of special schools and classes, led to the emergence of special education in Brazil, which was set up to cater exclusively for people with special needs and was a form of education that replaced ordinary education.

The history of special education in Brazil is marked by three periods: first by private initiatives aimed at meeting the interests of society, then by national initiatives with a welfare character, taken over by the federal government, and

---

[2] Special classes: these are classes that cater for students with severe cases of mental or multiple disabilities, within mainstream schools. It is important to note that, although they attend ordinary schools, they study in separate classrooms with a maximum of ten students (BRASIL, 2008, online).

[3] Resource rooms: these are educational rooms, staffed by a specialized teacher, which aim to complement the educational care provided in ordinary classes in the regular school system (BRASIL, 2008, online).

finally the current phase, which prioritizes the inclusion of people with disabilities in the regular education network.

Care for people with disabilities began with the Imperial Institute for Blind Children (now the Benjamin Constant Institute - IBC), in 1854, and three years later, in 1857, the Institute for Deaf Mutes (now the National Institute for Deaf Education - INES) was founded, both in Rio de Janeiro and according to Gugel (2008), these came about at the insistence of Dom Pedro II, who was emperor of Brazil at the time, and aimed to follow the European movement that Napoleon Bonaparte, emperor of France, had started, after stating that ex-soldiers were still useful and should therefore provide rehabilitation for people with disabilities through specific care.

Another fundamental milestone was the appearance, also in Rio de Janeiro, of an institution specializing in the care of people with mental disabilities, the Pestalozzi Institute, and in 1954 the Association of Parents and Friends of the Exceptional (APAE) was established.

Social policies in relation to special education in Brazil were influenced by international declarations and movements. In the 1940s, social demonstrations and family organizations in favour of people with disabilities began, with the Universal Declaration of Human Rights in 1948, which affirmed the right of everyone to education. It can be said that the development of Brazilian school inclusion of people with disabilities took place in 1961 with the Law of Guidelines and Bases of Education (Law No. 4.024/61), which guarantees the right of people with disabilities to be attended to preferentially within ordinary education.

In contradiction to this last law, Law No. 5.692/71 came into force in 1971. It reinforced the referral of students to special classes and schools, stating that the education system was not prepared to meet special educational needs.

In this context, there was no public policy for universal access to education, only special policies in relation to the education of students with disabilities, such as the creation of the National Center for Special Education - CENESP, by the MEC in 1973, responsible for the administration of special education in Brazil, which stimulated educational support for people with disabilities.

During this period, discussions about the rights of people with disabilities were being addressed worldwide, and 1981 was proclaimed the "International Year of Disabled People" by the United Nations, with the aim of encouraging the promotion of supports that value equality, rehabilitation and the prevention of disabilities.

Brazil also saw the creation in 1986 of the National Coordination for the Integration of People with Disabilities (CORDE), which is an agency of the Secretariat of State for Human Rights of the Ministry of Justice, responsible for managing policies aimed at integrating people with disabilities.

1.3 Special education and the challenge of inclusion

The Constitution is the highest law that organizes the State. The current Federal Constitution of Brazil was promulgated on October 5, 1988, which was extremely necessary, since the last one was promulgated in the middle of the Military Dictatorship, in 1967.

The period of the Military Regime was marked by indirect elections, armed forces with great power, workers without the right to strike, most decisions taken by the Executive Branch, among other things, but the crises in Brazil began to worsen, thus increasing the strength of the opposition parties and in 1984 in Praga da Se, in Sao Paulo, there was a movement with around 300,000 people who shouted "direct elections now", a year later Constitutional Amendment N. 25 was promulgated. A year later, Constitutional Amendment

No. 25 was enacted, which meant that the President would be elected by direct vote, beginning the re-democratization of the country, but this only really happened with the implementation of a new Federal Constitution in 1988 (RODRIGUES, 2006).

This new law is called the "Citizen's Constitution" and is a breakthrough for Brazilian society, as it has made significant changes to the previous one and was built with the help of society, setting limits on the power of rulers and defining the rights of citizens, be they individual, collective, social or political.

With regard to education, this Constitution establishes it as a right of all (art. 205), guaranteeing as a duty of the State the integration of schools and specialized educational assistance, taking place mainly in the regular school system (art. 208).

In the 1990s, discussions arose in Brazil about a new model of care for students, called school inclusion, as a counter-reaction to the process of integration, in which disabled students had to fit into the school's molds, without questioning the school's role. In the inclusive perspective, the school must adapt to the students, recognizing their differences and seeking new pedagogical practices that enable everyone to participate and progress. Therefore, the inclusive model starts to take place in special education in a different way to the integrationist model, but both have the same proposal, which is to include students with special educational needs in mainstream education.

In this context, the concept of inclusion becomes extremely important in special education, as it aims to assist all children, regardless of their differences, in ordinary education, with specialized educational assistance linked to the pedagogical proposal, taking place in the opposite period to classes, with the aim of helping to include not only people with disabilities, but all people with special educational needs.

It is important to emphasize that inclusive education includes special education, but cannot be confused with it. According to CNE/CEB Resolution No. 2, of September 11, 2001, in its article 3, special education means

> Art. 3
> [...] an educational process defined by a pedagogical proposal that ensures special educational resources and services, organized institutionally to support, complement, supplement and, in some cases, replace common educational services [...] (BRASIL, 2001, online).

while inclusive education proposes the participation of all students in regular education establishments and the school must cater for diversity, recognizing the uniqueness and needs of each one, thus guaranteeing the social integration and learning success of all.

In order for this proposal to come to fruition, it highlights the need for ongoing training for teachers and for resources to be earmarked for this training and for everyone to remain in school. From this perspective, the school needs to adapt to the specific characteristics of each student, offering quality education and building a new concept of the teaching and learning process, eliminating the segregationist character and guaranteeing the maximum development of those who, by right, should be included in this process.

It's important to note that public policies on inclusive education have had two fundamental milestones: the "World Conference on Education for All", which aimed to guarantee equal access to education for people with any type of disability, consolidated in 1994 in Jontiem, Thailand, and the Salamanca Declaration, drawn up at the "World Conference on Special Educational Needs", which took place in the city of Salamanca, Spain, in 1994, is based on the principle of welcoming everyone into the same classroom, regardless of their differences, promoting learning and meeting the needs of each individual. In order for this to be possible, it highlights the importance of applying resources in schools to guarantee quality care. This Declaration aims to reaffirm the right of all people to education, in accordance with the Universal Declaration of Human Rights of 1948.

As early as 1990, the Brazilian government enacted the Statute of the Child and Adolescent (Law No. 8.069/90), guaranteeing that

> Art. 3
> [...] children and adolescents enjoy all the fundamental rights inherent to the human person, without prejudice to the integral protection dealt with in this Law, being assured, by law or by other means, all the opportunities and facilities, in order to facilitate their physical, mental, moral, spiritual and social development, in conditions of freedom and dignity. (BRASIL, 1990, online)

In order to guide the process of school integration, the National Special Education Policy was introduced in 1994, which states that only those with disabilities who are able to keep up with normal students should have access to mainstream education. Therefore, it does not reform educational practices and does not value potential, keeping the responsibility for educating students with disabilities solely with special schools and classes.

Another fundamental highlight of special education in Brazil comes with the current Law of Guidelines and Bases of Education (LDB 9394/96) which, in chapter V, article 58, reaffirms what is stated in the 1988 Constitution, "preferential attendance in the regular school system", also guaranteeing when necessary: specialized support services in the regular school and depending on the severity of the student's disability, specialized educational care in special classes or schools, in addition to "[....] appropriate educational opportunities, taking into account the characteristics of the students, their interests, living and working conditions, through courses and examinations" (art. 37).

In 1999, Decree No. 3.298 defined special education as a complement to regular education at all levels of education, regulating Law No. 7.853/89 which "provides for the support of people with disabilities, their social integration [...]".

In 2001, the National Guidelines for Special Education in Basic Education (CNE/CEB n°2/2001) determined that all students must be enrolled and that it is the school's responsibility to ensure quality education for all. Complementing this idea, the National Education Plan (PNE) (Law n°10.172/2001) emphasizes that for inclusive education to be truly guaranteed, schools must adapt to meet human diversity.

The Brazilian government consented to the Guatemala Convention of May 28, 1999, through Decree No. 3.956/2001, which aims to eliminate all forms of discrimination or exclusion of people with disabilities by stating that everyone has the same rights. This Decree was an important advance in inclusive education, as it demanded a new interpretation of it, considering that any mainstream school that prevents people with disabilities from attending school would be discriminating against them.

In 2002, the National Curriculum Guidelines for the Training of Basic Education Teachers (CNE/CP n°1/2002) stipulated that the curriculum for teacher training should include knowledge aimed at meeting the diversity and specific needs of students with disabilities.

Also in 2002, through the promulgation of Law No. 10.436/02 and Ordinance No. 2.678/02, the Brazilian Sign Language and the Braille System were guaranteed, including the subject of Libras in the training of teachers and speech therapists, recommending both its use and the use of Braille throughout the country. Thus guaranteeing them as legal means of communication, expression and their dissemination in all teaching modalities.

Since 2003, the Brazilian government has given greater encouragement to the accessibility of students with disabilities in the regular school system, such as the Ministry of Education's Inclusive Education Program, which encourages the training of educators in order to guarantee everyone's right to access schooling and thus constitute an inclusive educational system.

The following year, the Federal Public Prosecutor's Office reaffirmed the right and importance of all people, with or without disabilities, to attend regular schools, through the document "The Access of Students with Disabilities to Schools and Common Classes in the Regular Network". That same year, President Luiz Inacio Lula da Silva signed Decree No. 5.296/04, which regulated Laws No. 10.048/00 and No. 10.098/00, with the former giving priority to people with physical disabilities, the elderly aged sixty-five or over, pregnant women, nursing mothers and people accompanied by infants and the latter determining standards and criteria for promoting accessibility for people with disabilities and, in this process, aiming to promote and support actions that make accessibility effective, the Accessible Brazil Program was created.

With regard to the inclusion of deaf people, Decree No. 5.626/05, which regulated Law No. 10.436/2002, emphasizes the importance of universities including Libras as a subject in their curricula, in order to prepare teachers, translators and instructors to assist these students in the mainstream.

In order to reinforce an inclusive education system, in 2006 the United Nations (UN) published the Convention on the Rights of Persons with Disabilities, which guarantees that people with disabilities are not excluded from free and compulsory education and that they are served in the regular network with the same quality as other students. This education must also provide aids and activities that enable the inclusion, access and permanence of students with special educational needs in higher education, according to the National Plan for Human Rights Education (2006), proposed by the Special Secretariat for Human Rights, the Ministry of Education, the Ministry of Justice and the United Nations Educational, Scientific and Cultural Organization (UNESCO).

Another important milestone in special education was the emergence of the Education Development Plan in 2007, which emphasizes the need for schools to have physical space that allows for accessibility, resource rooms and trained professionals for specialized educational care, with the aim of overcoming the conception of distance between regular education and special education, i.e. a single educational system that caters for social diversity.

In this context, the Commitment "All for Education" reaffirms the guarantee of access and permanence of people with disabilities in regular education and meeting their special educational needs, in order to encourage the process of inclusion, as stated in Decree No. 6.094/07.

1.3.1 National Policy on Special Education in Perspective Inclusive Education

All these aspects aimed at promoting and organizing inclusive education for people with disabilities in Brazil were regulated by the National Policy for Special Education from the Perspective of Inclusive Education (2008), which was triggered by the worldwide movement of political, cultural, social and pedagogical support. This policy was created by the Ministry of Education and the Special Education Secretariat in order to keep up with all the advances in this area, and so it includes all the legislation mentioned above.

It aims to build public policies in favor of regular education that caters for everyone, from early childhood education to higher education, promoting access, participation and learning without discrimination, and therefore determines priority funding for projects in institutions aimed at inclusive support and support for the regular education system for the inclusion of people with disabilities. The policy aims to guarantee:

- "Transversality of special education from early childhood education to higher education;"

- "Specialized educational assistance[4] ;"
- "Continuity of schooling at the highest levels of education;"
- "Training teachers for specialized educational care and other education professionals for school inclusion;"
- "Family and community involvement;"
- "Urban, architectural, furniture and equipment, transport, communication and information accessibility; and"
- "Intersectoral coordination in the implementation of public policies." (BRASIL, 2008, p. x).

According to the policy,

> [...] based on the references for the construction of inclusive educational systems, the organization of special schools and classes is being rethought, implying a structural and cultural change in the school so that all students have their specificities catered for (BRASIL, 2008, online).

In this way, special education emphasizes specialized educational care, offering the necessary resources and essential guidance within the ordinary school system. It is in this context that the policy directs its guidelines, so that this assistance is efficient in its function of developing and organizing the resources and ideal access according to the specificities of each student, highlighting the importance of this process being related to the pedagogical proposal of regular education.

This specialized educational service goes through different stages of learning, respecting the various stages of development. In early childhood education, it is done in a playful way, valuing the child through physical,

[4] Specialized Educational Assistance (AEE) was regulated by Decree No. 6.571/08, which emphasizes existing support for inclusive education and earmarks resources from the Basic Education Fund (Fundeb) to meet the specific needs of the segment.

emotional and cognitive stimuli and coexistence, because it is during this period that children "develop the necessary foundations for the construction of knowledge and the overall development of the student".

In the other cycles of education, which include primary education, higher education and youth and adult education, special attention is given according to the specific needs of the students, so that schooling opportunities are expanded, taking into account their learning possibilities and individual progress. In this context, the role of the teacher is fundamental to creating pedagogical strategies that provide quality teaching and ensure that students remain in school. This is why specific knowledge of the area is needed and why it is important to include this subject in the initial training of teachers and also in continuing training, as it is a subject that is currently much discussed and is gaining greater visibility every year.

The policy stresses the importance of the teacher in this process, but their work alone is insufficient. It is up to education systems to provide other professionals, such as instructors, translators and monitors, to help those with greater difficulties, especially in activities such as eating, moving around and hygiene. It should also promote projects in partnership with other areas, "aimed at architectural accessibility, health care, the promotion of social assistance, work and justice".

1.3.2 The Panorama of Inclusive Education in Brazil

The Ministry of Education (MEC) is a federal government body in Brazil, which was created in 1930 when Getulio Vargas came to power. It was called the "Ministry of Educational Affairs and Public Health" and carried out activities related to education, public health, sport and the environment. Until then, matters relating to education were dealt with by the "National Department of Education", linked to the Ministry of Justice.

In 1937, it was renamed the "Ministry of Education and Health", limiting its activities to education and health and this model lasted until 1953, when the federal government created the "Ministry of Health" and, with this autonomy given to the health area, the MEC - Ministry of Education and Culture - was officially created.

Also in 1937, a secretariat linked to this body was created, the Anisio Teixeira National Institute for Educational Studies and Research (INEP), which continues to exist and aims to carry out studies, research and evaluations on the Brazilian education system, in order to help formulate and implement public policies in the field of education.

The Brazilian educational model was centralized and organized by the MEC. With the first Law of Guidelines and Bases of Education (LDB) in 1961, the states and municipalities were given more autonomy, reducing the concentration of responsibilities in the MEC. With the new law in 1971, primary education became compulsory, with a diversified curriculum based on regional differences.

In 1985, the area of culture also gained autonomy, with the creation of the MinC (Ministry of Culture), leaving the MEC responsible only for education. Curiously, this acronym remains to this day, although it is now called the Ministry of Education.[5]

The MEC's activities became part of the National Education Policy in 1990, which encompasses education, civil teaching, university research and extension, teaching and special education.

In 1996, along with the creation of a new Education Guidelines and Bases Law (LDB), which includes early childhood education (nurseries and pre-school) and prioritizes the adequate training of basic education professionals (primary and secondary education), the Fund for the

[5] From 1992 to 1995, the MEC also became responsible for sport and was renamed the Ministry of Education and Sport.

Maintenance and Development of Primary Education (Fundef) came into existence, the Fund for the Maintenance and Development of Primary Education and the Valorization of Teaching Staff (Fundef) and ten years later (2006), it was replaced by the Fund for the Maintenance and Development of Basic Education and the Valorization of Education Professionals (Fundeb), thus benefiting the whole of basic education, from nursery school to secondary school. This is a commitment that the Union will make to basic education until 2020.

Along these lines, in 2007 the MEC also launched the Education Development Plan (PDE) to strengthen support for education and affirm the importance of investing in professional and higher education as a way of improving basic education.

After so many reforms, the MEC's current competencies, defined by Decree No. 4.791 of July 22, 2003, are: national education policy; early childhood education; education in general (primary education, secondary education, higher education, youth and adult education, professional education, special education and distance education, except military education); evaluation, information and educational research; and university research and extension.

This body, the Ministry of Education/National Institute for Educational Studies and Research (MEC/INEP), carries out the school census every year in all basic education schools and is able to monitor all enrollments throughout the federal, state, municipal and private networks. It also provides indicators of access for people with disabilities in ordinary classes, the provision of specialized educational care, accessibility in school buildings, training of qualified teachers, among others.

Although this body presents all this data, we would now like to highlight the number of people with disabilities enrolled in regular schools, as this is the focus of this research. It is extremely important to analyze the panorama of inclusive education in Brazil and in the state of São Paulo in order to gain a better understanding of the current context.

TABLE 1- Number of Enrolments of Students with Educational Needs Special Education in Regular Classes and/or Youth and Adult Education (MEC/INEP 2010)

	Private	Federal	State	Municipal	Total
Brazil	27.096	702	159.008	297.526	484.332
State of Sao Paulo	6.524	12	55.650	60.364	122.550

Source: Debora Maniglia and Tais Rodrigues Dib

In Brazil, 484,332 people with disabilities are enrolled in regular classes and/or in the EJA (Youth and Adult Education), of which 25.3% are in the state of Sao Paulo.

According to the table, the municipal network is the one with the most students with special educational needs enrolled, both in Brazil (61.4%) and in the state of Sao Paulo (49.25%).

TABLE 1 - Total Enrollment of People with Disabilities in the Regular School Network Education between 1998 and 2010 in Brazil (MEC/INEP 2010):

Year	1998	2002	2006	2010
Total enrollment	43.923	110.704	325.136	484.332

Source: Debora Maniglia and Tais Rodrigues Dib

The number of people with disabilities enrolled in mainstream schools has evolved greatly over the years. From 1998 to 2002 there was an increase of 66,781 students enrolled, from 2002 to 2006 there was a significant increase, 214,432 enrolments in this period. From 2006 to 2010, there was an increase of 159,196 enrolments. In twelve years, the increase was 440,409, a factor that may have contributed to this growth was the expansion of laws regulating access and permanence of all in school, without discrimination and the constant discussions on the subject.

It is worth pointing out that an increase in the number of students enrolled is not enough for inclusion to happen, so in the next chapter we will highlight the conditions necessary for students to remain in school, emphasizing, among other things, the importance of initial and continuing training for teachers and education professionals, who ultimately make the proposal for inclusive education feasible, offering support to meet the individual needs of each student.

CHAPTER 2 THE NECESSARY CONDITIONS FOR THE OPERATIONALIZATION OF INCLUSIVE EDUCATION FOR PEOPLE WITH DISABILITIES

2.1 School from the perspective of including people with disabilities

In view of the current discussions on inclusive education, it is important to emphasize the need to create mechanisms for obtaining quality care, with physical adaptations and new pedagogical practices that enable students to participate effectively in school, in all its senses, educational, social and emotional, in addition to the integral development of each one.

According to Figueiredo (2008), the inclusive school values the knowledge that each student brings with them so that together they can build new knowledge and solve the difficulties encountered in the classroom. The author also states that this teaching model focuses on the difficulties of the inclusion process in the school and not on the particular characteristics of the students, so that the school must be dynamic and able to develop different responses to the different rhythms of learning so that it can implement in the institution what is already guaranteed by law, developing new values in its environment and thus contributing to the achievement of a less unequal and more democratic society.

In this context, two aspects are essential in the organization of educational institutions in order to provide quality education: accessibility and pedagogical practices. In order for students to attend mainstream schools with autonomy and independence, they must first have adequate facilities. According to Rebelo (2004), it should be noted that students who attend well-designed schools have, on average, significantly better performance than those who attend schools with poor architecture.

Thus, as the National Policy on Special Education from the perspective of Inclusive Education states, it is important that measures are taken to make it possible to adapt the school environment and eliminate existing physical, pedagogical and social barriers within the school context, such as access ramps, adapted toilets, interpreters of Brazilian Sign Language (LIBRAS), transcription of texts into Braille for those with cerebral palsy and, above all, teacher training, adapted toilets, interpreters of the Brazilian Sign Language (LIBRAS), transcription of texts into Braille, alternative communication for those with cerebral palsy and, above all, teacher training to develop intervention strategies that facilitate the implementation of the inclusive proposal.

Legislation highlights education as a right for all, guaranteeing access to and permanence in compulsory, free and quality education, as proposed by the 1988 Federal Constitution, so participation in all the activities carried out at school and the possibility of communication and interaction within the school group are fundamental to successful learning. This requires the creation of physical, environmental and material conditions, such as those mentioned above, as well as appropriate furniture, specific resources and equipment for use in the classroom, adequate lighting and possibilities for movement.

According to Carvalho (2010), it is worth highlighting some points that are relevant to the management of inclusive schools, such as: developing cultures, policies and practices that favor this process, providing learning according to the student's special educational needs, creating spaces for teachers to exchange experiences, respecting individual differences, valuing educational work, seeking the necessary resources for quality education, among others. The aforementioned author emphasizes that the school cannot only be thought of as a space for socializing and living together, but also as building knowledge, respecting individuality and identity in order to enable the development of students' personalities and thus allow autonomy and confidence, especially for those with some kind of disability. It is also up to this institution to uphold democratic ideals, in other words, to offer the same opportunities that everyone needs in order to exercise citizenship and remove barriers to learning and participation for all.

Therefore, a school environment that proposes inclusive education embraces diversity, allowing all students, with or without disabilities, to occupy the same space and have the same educational experiences. This proposal stimulates coexistence, the exchange of experiences, respect and appreciation of each individual, making it possible for differences to become familiar, in other words, for this diversity to be seen in a common way.

Through administration, planning and execution, this new educational model provides for everyone to remain in regular education, with effective proposals for the work of the professionals involved, valuing their relationship with the student, respecting the different conceptions, cultures, ethnicities, principles and orientations in accordance with current legislation, consequently, the school provides interaction, independence, socialization, education and learning, basic principles for the implementation of quality education.

Regarding pedagogical support,

> [...] the teacher's role in the classroom is extremely important, as it guides teaching practice in a creative way, seeking to adapt content and pedagogical materials so that students learn according to their possibilities and their time, thus facilitating the participation of all and valuing individual identity, thus benefiting not only those with special educational needs, but everyone involved (CARVALHO, 2010).

Based on this, we will highlight the importance of this professional training in the next section.

2.2 Training educators for Inclusive Education

The concept of an inclusive school "proposes a way of organizing the educational system that takes into account the needs of all students and is structured according to those needs" (MANTOAN, 2006). This reformulation proposed by inclusive education, which is so much discussed and addressed today, is essential for respecting diversity and guaranteeing learning that meets the specific needs of each individual.

Education is considered fundamental in the formation of more autonomous, critical and reflective citizens. Consequently, the teacher plays an extremely important role in the construction of knowledge, especially for students with special educational needs, in order to guarantee their independence and permanence in the regular school system.

In this way, several aspects are essential for the implementation of this inclusive educational model, highlighting that teacher training must be directed in this direction. As Reis (2006) states, it is important for teachers to know how to deal with individual characteristics (abilities, interests, experiences, etc.) and to create pedagogical practices that match this information and needs.

From this perspective, some flexibility is needed in the classroom, which leads teachers to act creatively in terms of adapting the physical environment, the content so that students learn according to their possibilities, respecting each one's time and the resources to obtain new teaching materials in order to facilitate learning and participation, benefiting not only those with some kind of disability, but the whole group of students.

Teachers are now taking on greater responsibilities, valuing the socialization and participation of students, in a way that emphasizes a more humane education without injustice and exclusion and, in this way, forming more respectful, critical, creative and autonomous citizens, This is a difficult task, because the training they received was reproductive, the mere transmission of knowledge, the absence of theories for working with people with disabilities and they always had the practice of giving planned lessons, as if there was already a "right formula" (SEGATE, 2010).

These elements point to the need for teacher training to enable them to meet the challenges posed by this new model of education and, according to Reis (2006), this change must take place from the initial training stage onwards, since it is during this period that the future professional becomes familiar with the situations they are likely to face and, to this end, it is interesting to expand and improve the discussions related to this issue in all the subjects of the course, so that teaching practice is more complete. However, this training alone is not enough for the pedagogical project to be carried out in accordance with inclusive principles; professional action in a reflective and collective manner contributes significantly to this situation. According to Rodrigues (2006), the development of skills for inclusive education can only be acquired through in-service practice.

Therefore, although this initial stage is essential, the professional must not be restricted to it alone, but must extend to continuing training and the intense search for new knowledge, in order to keep up with the demands that arise in society, so that

This, according to Segate (2010), should not just be a personal desire of the professional, but a political-pedagogical project of the schools.

> Teacher training has to be seen as a continuous process based on the perspective of growth, which means that teacher training cannot be understood simply as a sum of specific subjects + pedagogical subjects, but must take place throughout the initial training course and extend continuously, valuing professional experience by considering the teacher in the personal, professional and knowledge-producing dimensions translated into a continuous process of learning to learn (KULLOK, 2000, p.18).

Carvalho (2010) highlights the importance of a researcher's spirit in this professional training, of recording the experiences that went right and wrong in the classroom, because everyday experiences also strengthen professional training and sharing this with the professional category is very important, The author also emphasizes that, as a researcher, professional practice would be more pleasurable, as their routine at school would have an investigative character and would stimulate their critical spirit.

As an alternative to continuing training, there are extra training courses, cited by Mantoan (2006), with a shorter duration and favorable content that make it possible to add new knowledge and updates, but the author stresses that these courses must meet the real needs of the professionals.

In addition to specializations in the area, teacher training should include interdisciplinary experience, teamwork, research, the creation of acting techniques and reflection on the values of education, considering various possibilities for change according to the demands of the students and thus promoting quality teaching that enables the formation of critical, autonomous, creative and independent students (SEGATE, 2010).

In 2005, the Ministry of Education and the Department of Special Education created the document "Subsidiario a Politica de Inclusao", which aims to help transform schools into inclusive, quality spaces, emphasizing the importance of teacher training in this process.

This document emphasizes the promotion of discussion groups among teachers so that experiences can be exchanged and considers it enriching to have professionals from other areas participate, who can present different opinions and that this interdisciplinarity should not only take place within the school context, but also in an interlocution with other institutions, which may be in the area of health, assistance, etc.

He also points out that, up until 2005, there had been very few experiences of institutions that relied on this support from other professionals.

In this perspective, the schools are alluding to a broader team, made up of: neurologists, occupational therapists, psychologists, psychiatrists, speech therapists and social workers. The desire for a more complete team would be that, with the combination of knowledge, it could facilitate the students' learning and ease the pressure suffered by teachers in the process of inclusion. According to the document, this team would also monitor families and students, even making home visits, identify the specific needs of the school, carry out investigations in the community in order to identify specialized services in the network that could be linked to school services and mediate between the classroom and specialized educational care.

Finally, it is clear from the document that this process of inclusion should not be restricted to the teacher-student, but also involves an effort by the entire school community, social segments and families to identify impediments and look for alternatives, thus constituting the inclusion movement and the consolidation of the inclusive educational model.

CHAPTER 3 THE INCLUSION OF STUDENTS WITH DISABILITIES IN REGULAR MUNICIPAL EDUCATION IN FRANCA/SP

3.1 Contextualizing the municipal education network of the municipality of Franca

The municipality of Franca is located in the interior of the state of Sao Paulo. Its population in 2010 was 318,239 (according to the IBGE/2010) and it is known throughout Brazil as "The Capital of Men's Shoes", as it is the largest producer of shoes in Brazil and Latin America. It has more than a thousand large and medium-sized industries, so this sector is very important for the economy of the municipality.

According to data from the Franca Municipal Department of Education, the city has a literacy rate of 96.37% (May 2010) and it is important to note that the percentage of children (7 to 14 years old) out of school is zero%, so there are no children who are not served by the network, with the exception of cases of truancy during the school year, which is reported to the Child and Youth Guardianship Councils.

Franca's municipal school system covers kindergarten (nursery schools and EMEIs - Municipal Schools for Kindergarten) and elementary school (EMEBs - Municipal Schools for Basic Education), youth and adult education (EJA) and the Integrated Education Center (CEI):

- Early childhood education comprises nurseries (0 to 3 years) and EMEIs (pre-school/4 and 5 years), and primary education is offered by EMEBs up to the 5th grade;
- EJA can be face-to-face, offered by units in some neighborhoods, or

semi-presential by Capao for young people and adults;

- CEI is a project that caters for adolescents (over fourteen) and adults with mental or multiple disabilities, providing work activities to prepare them for inclusion in the job market.

According to data from Franca City Hall, in 2008 there were 19,815 pupils enrolled in public education in Franca (45% in the municipal network and 55% in the state network), of these 2,161 were in nursery school, 6,971 were in pre-school, 9,693 were in elementary school and 990 in secondary school and in 2011, the municipal network had:

- 42 day-care centers with 4,193 students enrolled and 2 municipal day-care centers with 220 children;
- 39 EMEIs with 6,802 students;
- 28 EMEBs serving 10,522 students;
- EJA - 5 face-to-face schools, with 582 students in elementary school (6th to 9th grade) and 1,149 students in secondary school;
- CESUM - 1 semi-presential school serving 229 students in elementary school and 459 in secondary school;
- Literacy for young people and adults, with 24 centers offered three times a week to 700 students.

The municipal network currently serves 401 people with disabilities in this regular education network (with the exception of nursery schools), 200 of whom have a medical report. In nursery schools, the number of students included in 2010 was 28 (this figure has not yet been calculated for 2011). This figure is considered low compared to the number of children enrolled (4,413 - affiliated nursery schools and municipal nursery schools), given that at this age most of the children attend APAE (Association of Parents and Friends of the

Exceptional), which aims to stimulate, start the educational process and refer them to elementary school when the student is ready.

For the care of children with special educational needs, the municipal network has five resource rooms located in the different regions of the city and the creation of five more is planned for 2012.

3.2 The research setting: a primary school

The "Escola Municipal de Educapao Basica Sueli Contini Marques" was the educational institution where we carried out our research. It is located at Rua Mamede Silva, 2771, in the Tropical I neighborhood, in the northern region of Franca, a place considered peripheral in the city.

The school is an elementary school from 1st to 5th grade, with 619 students enrolled, twelve in the morning and twelve in the afternoon. Of these pupils, six have disabilities, so only 0.96% of the total number of pupils. There is no resource room in the school, but one is due to be set up next year, and the materials have already arrived.

In order to understand how the process of inclusion takes place in this school, we interviewed four teachers who have these students in their classrooms, as well as the pedagogue and the pedagogical coordinator. These subjects were identified by fictitious flower names: Violet, Daisy, Rose, Jasmine, Bromelia and Orchid.

3.3 Inclusive education in Franca/SP: the expectations of educators

3.3.1 Profile of the subjects

TABLE 3 - Profile

Fictitious name	Function	Age	Sex	Training	Ano de Conclusion Training	Working Time	Time working with Inclusive Education
Violet	Pedagogue	44 years old	female	top	1997	27 years old	27 years old
Daisy	Teacher	33 years old	female	top	2000	12 years old	7 years
Pink	Coordinator	41 years old	female	top	1995	18 years old	6 years
Jasmine	Teacher	34 years old	female	top	2000	15 years	4 years
Bromelia	Teacher	35 years old	female	top	1998	15 years	15 years
Orchid	Teacher	45 years old	female	top	1989	18 years old	3 years

Source: Debora Maniglia and Tais Rodrigues Dib

It is worth noting that the professionals are all female, aged between 33 and 45. They all have higher education and have studied pedagogy at private universities.

As for the period of training, 50% graduated in the 1990s, they have been working in the field of education for between 12 and 15 years, 33% have been working in the field for 18 years and one, 16.6%, has been working in education for 27 years.

With regard to the length of time they have been working with inclusive education, 33% of the professionals surveyed have been working for between 3 and 4 years; 33% for between 6 and 7 years; one of the professionals (16.6%) has been working in the area for 15 years and another (16.6%) has been working in this area for around 27 years.

Only 33% have been working with inclusive education since they entered the field and the rest of the professionals (66.6%) have been working with inclusion for 7 years or less. We believe that the majority have been working in this area for less than a decade because during this period there has been an increase in the number of people with disabilities enrolled in the regular school system, as shown by the MEC data.

And it's worth noting that, at this juncture, many professionals end up going through new experiences, which causes insecurity at work and a need for change in the school context. This gave rise to an interest in understanding the perspective of professionals in this inclusive process, the difficulties encountered and the possible contribution of the Social Worker in this space.

3.3.2 The limits and possibilities of including students with disabilities: from the point of view of educators

Giving a voice to the educators involved in the subject under study: inclusive education for students with disabilities and recognizing their importance in the process of implementing the new paradigm of inclusion, although we are aware that this is one of the aspects that interact in the implementation of this policy of educational inclusion.

In order to interpret the information obtained through the interviews, we categorized the different themes addressed as follows: professional training; the types of disability the students have; then we tried to understand the concept of inclusion that the educators have and, finally, we addressed the contribution of the social worker in the educational area according to the view of these professionals.

With regard to the **training of the professionals**, the majority report having studied beyond graduation in order to be able to work better with inclusion, such as teacher Margarida, who of those interviewed is the most qualified in the area:

> I have a postgraduate degree in Mental Disability, at the time it was mental disability, now it's intellectual, I have a degree in Psychopedagogy which I think gives me a lot of grounding to work with intellectual disability and I've recently done an adaptation, which

> is Intellectual Disability in Inclusion, in the Inclusive Perspective (Margarida).

It's important to note that this teacher also works at APAE, a factor that may have influenced her greater interest in the subject and we can also infer that, having worked in this institution specializing in the field of disability, she felt the need to invest in her training.

Despite the fact that the educators have been trained, 50% said that they were unaware of any courses offered by the municipal network that are directly related to special education:

> [...] I didn't have the opportunity within the school, I was the one who went after it, but it was also because I worked in education that was already geared towards the disabled, so it was more on my part. (Margarida)
>
> I wasn't invited to any of them (Orchid).
>
> I've been in the municipal system for three years now and I haven't had a course directly on this subject, I haven't. (Bromelia).

However, the pedagogue, the coordinator and only one of the teachers stated that the network offers courses, but at times that may not be suitable for those who work two shifts:

> The town hall offers, it always looks for courses for those who are interested, because there are teachers who have students with inclusion and who can't always attend a course, sometimes because they work two periods they can't attend the course, but the town hall always offers these courses. (Jasmine)

We understand that the lack of access to complementary courses for all professionals is an element that hinders the process of educational inclusion. As we pointed out in the previous chapter, extra courses, of short duration, but objective and with quality content, can add new knowledge and updates, according to Mantoan (2006).

With regard to the **types of disability** present at the school, we found that the main one is intellectual disability. Of the six students who attend this institution, all have this type of disability, but some have another disability associated with it, as the pedagogue explains:

> Two children with CP, cerebral palsy, I have a child with clipel syndrome, which is a mental illness, and another child who also has CP, but with motor skills, let me see if there are any others I've forgotten, and another child who has mental retardation. (Violeta)

We would like to highlight the work of APAE, which stimulates children with intellectual disabilities from birth in order to help them develop better and sends them to mainstream education when they are ready. This work receives the help of the town hall, through a pedagogue who goes to APAE every week to help with the work and analyze those who are already qualified to attend regular school.

The municipality also has an Association of Families, People and People with Cerebral Palsy, called "Projeto Caminhar", which provides therapeutic care in the areas of: Phonoaudiology, Physiotherapy, Psychotherapy, Psychopedagogy and Social Work, with the aim of improving the quality of life of those who attend. This project also helps education professionals in the municipal school system, as Jasmim, a teacher, pointed out.

It is worth pointing out that these two projects help to include people with intellectual disabilities in mainstream education, but in different ways: the first project prioritizes care before they enter the mainstream system and the second works in conjunction with it.

Regarding the **concept of educational inclusion**, the professionals approached the subject in different ways. The pedagogue and the coordinator were closer to the concept of inclusion set out in the legislation, which according to the National Policy for Special Education in the Perspective of Inclusive Education is "[...] access, participation and learning of students with disabilities [...] in regular schools, guiding the education systems to promote responses to special educational needs". These professionals emphasized that they aim to serve students according to what they really need for effective learning, respecting each one's time.

We believe that the fact that the pedagogue and the coordinator have a more scientific knowledge of the subject is related to their greater participation in the courses offered by the municipality that deal with special education legislation.

Ms. Orquidea stressed the importance of professionals being better prepared to receive these children. Teacher Bromelia related this practice only to socialization. Teacher Jasmine reported the difficulties she faced in the classroom, especially in relation to the number of students.

We would like to emphasize teacher Margarida, who presented the concept of inclusive education in a more comprehensive way, perhaps because she has studied the subject more extensively:

> I think that in the field of social inclusion it's very interesting, because I believe that every person has to be respected, regardless of their difficulties, because everyone has difficulties in life, and I think that respect between people is a value that I preserve the most, inclusion at school isn't easy, because of all the changes the school has to go through, but it's necessary, I don't believe that every child with a disability, those with very severe disabilities, the school today isn't prepared, unfortunately, but it has to prepare itself, Today I don't think it's going to happen in a way that's suitable for the child, they may even receive it, but I have my doubts about whether the teacher will be prepared, whether there will be a team in the school to support them, this will have to change and I think it will, I hope it will, but with a lot of respect, with a lot of responsibility, inclusion is a question of responsibility, everyone from the family, the school, the administration, society, everyone, if it happens, if it's going to happen, let it be done with a lot of responsibility.(Margarida)

In order for people with disabilities to learn successfully, we know how important it is to have resources available to meet their needs. Although the teachers emphasized that they didn't have enough resources, they said that they used their creativity to develop effective teaching proposals, achieving satisfactory student development.

> In my case, with my student, I see progress in him, but he doesn't have the same development as other students. Ideally, for example, in the case of my student, who has cerebral palsy, he would need more manual tools, because he doesn't have fine motor coordination yet, right? so he would need a few more resources, which can often be a bit more expensive for the system, so I try to substitute, mobile alphabets, because even though he's in fifth grade he's still learning to read, so I use some resources like mobile alphabets, figures that help him in this literacy process.
> So there are resources, but we still need a bit more. (Jasmine)

Inclusive education, according to Correia (1997), proposes a school institution that is able to attend to children as a whole, considering their main levels of development (academic, socio-emotional and personal), in order to guarantee a quality education. The professionals agree that this process takes place within the school, but only from the perspective of socialization and not giving significant importance to learning. Once again, we would like to highlight teacher Margarida, who showed the greatest visibility on the subject, also emphasizing the importance of involving other professionals:

> As far as the classroom is concerned, inclusion is very peaceful, it contributes to the student's social development, but I also believe that in order to have cognitive development, for it to be integral, it has to have other resources, it has to have something more, school alone doesn't guarantee its integral development, as much as he creates strategies to guarantee that learning, there are deficiencies, there are conditions in which the child needs other support, which suddenly the school, a period of her class doesn't guarantee, I think she needs something more to have this integral development, speech therapy, physio, other resources have to be guaranteed, the school alone isn't enough.(Margarida)

Complementing this question, the professionals highlight socializing as a positive point and are unanimous in reporting the lack of teacher training as the main difficulty encountered in the learning process:

> The positive thing is what I told you about socialization, their participation, the respect they have for each other, and the negative thing I think is the teacher's lack of preparation to work with these children. (Orchid)

> [...] teachers had to be better prepared on how to work with some special cases that occur and this is a new policy, inclusion is being talked about now, so it's something new for us, both for teachers and managers and let's say that we are going through a process of experience and everything that is new is not easy, so as a teacher I feel this, we look for ways, look for resources, exchange ideas so that this child feels welcomed and can develop. (Bromelia)

We observed that despite not having the necessary support to work with students with disabilities, the teachers were very dedicated and committed to creating pedagogical strategies that help individual learning.

In view of all these statements made by the research subjects, it was clear that they believe in including people with disabilities in the regular school system, not just to comply with legislation, but also to contribute to the student's all-round development.

Regarding the **work of the social worker**, although they were unaware of this professional's duties in the educational area, due to the absence of social work in this policy, they consider it important to participate in order to make this inclusive policy effective, highlighting the interlocution between the family and the school as an essential factor, as well as associating the work of the social worker with the search to guarantee children's rights:

> I really believe that the social worker could, all of a sudden, help these families in the sense of even looking for their rights in relation to the benefits they could get, so, for example, I see the mother of this particular student of mine trying to get a resource, which would have

> to be available to her financially and she can't get it, so I really believe that a social worker would help direct this family a little better, giving guidance, even within the home and looking for these resources. (Jasmine)

> Of course, in my opinion, there are many families who don't know what they can do, for example, so that that child can develop, as I said before, within their potential, so the main job of the social service would be to guide, to look within the municipality, or even a state agency, what help that child can have, if it's psychological, if it's physical, then what the municipality, or even the school can offer, or even look for a resource to guide the professionals who have direct contact with these children. (Bromelia)

It's worth noting that the pedagogue mentioned the need for liaison with other care networks, attributing this to the role of the social worker. She also considers that she often ends up performing functions that would be carried out by a social work professional:

> [...] I think the Social Work professional could be contributing, making the connection between education and health, to help. [...] I'm a great believer in Social Work, in fact, I think that I, for example, as a pedagogue, do a lot of the work of a social worker, you know, the guidance counselor ends up doing it too, but it's something that we've always asked for in our meetings at the Municipal Office and we really believe that there should be a psychologist, a social worker, brought from the health area to education, to work there together, as a team with us. (Violeta)

The document Subsidiario a Politica de Inclusão (2005), cited in the second chapter, highlights the importance of this interlocution between education and other institutions, such as health and care, which is in line with the pedagogue's opinion.

In this context, we believe that the effective work of the Social Worker is fundamental, helping to make inclusive education a reality, seeking to transform the reality presented in an action that involves the entire community in which the school is inserted, as Lamamoto (2001) states:

> [...] requires the social worker to participate as a professional subject who has the competence to propose and negotiate with the institution on their projects, to defend their field of work, their professional qualifications and functions [...] to develop their ability to decipher reality and build creative work proposals capable of preserving and making rights effective, based on the demands that emerge in everyday life. [...] and seek to grasp the movement of reality in order to detect trends and possibilities within it.

According to the results obtained from the field research, we believe that the inclusion of a social worker in the school team is essential, as it would bring significant contributions to the students and to the school-family-community relationship. In this respect, we consider it important to make a note of the following item, since the intervention of the Social Worker in this area is still little known and is in the process of being built up.

3.4 Possible interventions for social workers in the field of education

It is extremely important to understand that in Brazil, in the social and economic sphere, within a globalized world, competitive, exclusionary relationships predominate and people are increasingly taking a utilitarian view, due to the current mode of production, capitalism, which prioritizes the economic over the social, leaving parts of society in subhuman conditions, a model where people do not have the same opportunities (MARGAREZI, 2010).

As a result, according to Amaro (1997), relationships at school are generally hierarchical, characterized by indifference, a dispute over who knows best, a lack of dialogue prevailing, and marked only by incoherent attitudes and postures. As a result, students are the ones who suffer the most, as they are influenced by their own emotions and are left unmotivated and uncommitted.

The same authors also point out that there are other factors that contribute to the disintegration of school as a space for joint growth, since the current living conditions of a large section of society have been greatly affected by this exclusionary mode of production, emphasizing that children with precarious social conditions and exposed to situations of vulnerability find it more difficult to learn.

We can see that the educational proposal, from an inclusive perspective, tends to suffer impacts within the current capitalist model, which is, above all, exclusionary, and this is a rich field for the work of the social worker, so much so that we noticed, through the school professionals, that they recognize that there are social demands that call for the specific technical work of the Social Work professional, therefore the inclusion of this professional in the collective work developed by the school team. They also highlight the role of the Social Worker in the school-family coordination process and the child, adolescent and family protection network, facilitating institutional relations and mobilizing the participation of the user population.

In order to meet the demands of the school and help inclusion to take place in the best possible way, the institution needs to be not only physically fit, but also have an adequate team of human resources.

> Contribute to the entry, return, permanence and success of children and adolescents in school; encourage the family-school-community relationship by expanding the space for their participation in school, including them in the educational process; broaden the social vision of those involved in education, decoding social issues; provide articulation between education and other social policies and third sector organizations, establishing partnerships, facilitating the school community's access to their rights. (MARTINS, 1999, p. 60)

Thus, the social worker is the professional trained to

> Improve the living conditions and survival of families and students; open up channels for subjects to interfere in the school's decision-making processes (class councils); expand the collection of information and knowledge about social issues in the school

> community; stimulate the experience and learning of the democratic process within the school and with the community; strengthen collective actions; carry out research that can contribute to the analysis of the social reality of the students and their families; maximize the use of community resources; and contribute to the professional training of new social workers, providing an internship field that is suited to the new demands of the professional profile. (MARTINS, 1999, p.70)

According to Amaro (1997), the challenges imposed on society today increasingly require a united effort to solve them, hence the importance of a larger team in schools to exchange information and experiences and complement each other in order to deal with the multiplicity of differences in which they find themselves and to give students with disabilities the possibility of developing tasks that are common to other students.

Another important contribution, according to Lamamoto (1998), is that the Social Worker acts in society by exercising socio-educational functions, and at school it couldn't be any different. This work aims to make people reflect on everyday issues of class, gender, ethnicity, cultural values, among others, so that they can act more critically, politically and respectfully towards society.

Martins (2009) also highlights the contribution of the social worker in a process of continuous training for school staff, reflecting on issues such as domestic violence, drugs, poverty and the legislative instruments that guide the care of students, such as the Statute of the Child and Adolescent. The author states that in order for professionals to have coherent practices in the school environment, they need to investigate and analyze the reality in which the school is located, so that they can even help build a pedagogical project that better meets the needs of those it serves.

The Social Worker is a fundamental professional in working to guarantee rights in the school environment and to ensure people's citizenship. He or she works in conjunction with the team and other institutions to find intervention strategies, thus improving the teaching-learning relationship for all students and, above all, helping to include people with disabilities in the regular school system.

The municipality of Franca has seven Social Workers who work in the Department of Education. Due to the small number of professionals and considering the breadth of the educational network, they work in schools indirectly and specifically with the early childhood education units. The projects developed are: the Bolsa Familia Program School Presence Project, the Adopt a University Student Project, the Popular Courses Project, the University Scholarship Program and the Visual School Health Program.

According to Martins (2007), some municipalities in the state of São Paulo have social workers who work specifically with special education, such as Osasco, Embu, Maua and Hortolandia: Osasco, Embu, Maua and Hortolandia. However, the number of Social Work experiences in the area of special education and inclusive education is small, despite the fact that the contribution of this professional in this area is important and significant.

Finally, it is a great challenge to point out that the Social Worker has an important contribution to make in the field of educational inclusion, working with families and as part of a multidisciplinary team, uncovering the expressions of the social question that directly reflect on the students' development at school and, above all, in the articulation of public policies.

FINAL CONSIDERATIONS

The aim of this study was to understand the process of educational inclusion of people with disabilities from the perspective of professionals working in the field, taking a municipal primary school in the city of Franca/SP as a snapshot of reality. In this context, presenting the historical trajectory, the legislation, the importance of teacher training, among other aspects that are essential for inclusion to take place, was extremely important in order to deepen the theoretical knowledge on the subject of the work and make it possible to interpret the results obtained in the field research.

From the reflections in this study, it is clear that inclusive education represents a fundamental space for social transformation and that the school plays an essential role in guaranteeing quality education for all, accepting and valuing differences and diversity. Believing in the benefits of this new educational model and in the capacity of all children to develop and learn, we carried out our research.

As a result of the analysis of the information obtained, we realized that inclusion represents a challenge for the professionals involved, who build up knowledge to work with students, aiming for educational inclusion, which occurs mainly through practice and daily experiences, respecting individualities and meeting the needs of each one.

We emphasize the importance of initial and continuing teacher training, the availability of courses offered by the government and the promotion of spaces dedicated to sharing these experiences as key aspects in the success of learning and the integral development of students with some kind of disability, be it intellectual, visual or hearing.

Although the schools do not have all the necessary resources to receive students with special educational needs, i.e. they still don't offer enough professional training courses, the elimination of architectural barriers, fewer students in the classroom, teaching resources and materials, among other factors, inclusion has already begun and the teachers are in the process of building methods and strategies to make this educational process effective. It is therefore hoped that the institution will be a place where there is no form of discrimination or prejudice, respect for differences and appreciation of each person's learning time.

The role of the Social Worker in this context of school inclusion is essential, in guaranteeing the rights of people with disabilities, providing guidance to families, interlocuting with other networks, such as health and welfare, acting through their knowledge of social reality and the repercussions of the social issue that significantly interfere in the development of students, with a focus on seeking the joint participation of society in these supports.

An interdisciplinary team working in education makes it possible to glimpse true inclusion, as it provides greater possibilities for action, by overcoming this challenge and believing in the potential of those with special educational needs, and thus broadening the strategies and support undertaken.

In this way, inclusive education ceases to be just an aspect guaranteed by legislation and educational documents and becomes an important step in a journey of struggles and movements in the search for the same chances of living together, studying, working, leisure and, finally, opportunities to access all the goods produced socially for this segment of the population who are also subjects of rights.

REFERENCES

ALVES, J.A. O Planejamento de Pesquisa Qualitativas em Educapao. **Caderno de Pesquisas**, Sao Paulo, n. 77, p. 55, 1991.

AMARO, Sarita Teresinha Alves. **Servipo Social na escola:** o encontro da realidade com a educapao. Porto Alegre: Sagra Luzzatto, 1997.

BARDIN, L **Content analysis**. Translated by Luis Antero Reto and Augusto Pinheiro. 70. ed. Lisbon: Martins Fontes, 1977.

BRAZIL. Law n. 8.069, of July 13, 1990. Provides for the Statute of Children and Adolescents and other measures. **Diario Oficial da Uniao**, July 16, 1990. Available at: <http://www.planalto.gov.br/ccivil_03/Leis/L8069.htm> Accessed in November 2010.

BRASIL. Law n. 9.394, of December 20, 1996. **Establishes the guidelines and bases of national education.** Available at: <http://www.planalto.gov.br/ccivil_03/Leis/L9394.htm> Accessed on: 02. nov. 2010.

BRAZIL. Ministry of Education. Special Education Secretariat. **Direito a educapao:** necessidades educacionais especiais: subsidios para atuapao do ministerio publico brasileiro. Brasilia, DF: MEC/SEESP, 2001.

BRAZIL. Ministry of Education. **Política Nacional de Educapao Especial na Perspectiva da Educapao Inclusiva.** Brasilia: MEC/SEEP, 2008. Available at: <http://portal.mec.gov.br/seesp/arquivos/pdf/politica.pdf>. Accessed on: May 15, 2011.

BRAZIL. Presidency of the Republic. Constitution (1988). **1988 Federative Constitution of Brazil:** promulgated in 1988. Available at: <http://www.planalto.gov.br/ccivil_03/constituicao/constitui%C3%A7ao.htm>. Accessed on: 01. nov. 2010.

BRAZIL. **CNE/CEB Resolution n°02.** Establishes National Guidelines for Special Education in Basic Education. Brasilia. 2001.

CARVALHO, Rosita Edler. **Inclusive Education:** what are we talking about? 2005. Available at: <http://www.fcee.sc.gov.br/index.php?option=com_docman&task=doc_view&gid=238> . Accessed on: 16. nov. 2010.

CARVALHO, Rosita Edler. **Inclusive education:** putting the "is" in "is". Porto Alegre: Mediagao, 2010.

CORREIA, L. M. **Alunos com necessidades educativas especiais nas classes regulares.** Porto: Porto Editora, 1997.

DINIZ, Debora. **What is disability**. Sao Paulo: Brasiliense, 2007.

FERREIRA, Moura Elisa Caputo; GUIMARAES, Marly. **Inclusive Education.** Rio de Janeiro: DP&A, 2003.

FIGUEIREDO, R. V. **Gestao da aprendizagem na diversidade:** relatorio de pesquisa. Fortaleza: Federal University of Ceara, 2008.

GUGEL, Maria Aparecida. **People with disabilities and their relationship with human history.** 2008.

IAMAMOTO, Marilda Vilela. **O Servigo Social na contemporaneidade:** trabalho e formação. 7. ed. Sao Paulo: Cortez, 1998.

IBGE. Developed by the Brazilian Institute of Geography and Statistics. Available
at: <http://www.ibge.gov.br>. Accessed on: July 10, 2011.

KOSIK, Karel. **Dialectics of the Concrete.** Rio de Janeiro: Paz e Terra, 1976.

KULLOK, Maisa Gomes Brandao. **The demands of teacher training today.** Maceio: EDUFAL, 2000.

MANTOAN, Maria Teresa Egler. Pedagogical paths of inclusive education. In: GAIO, Roberta; MENEGHETI, Rosa (Org.). **Caminhos pedagogicos da educagao especial.** 4. ed. Petropolis, RJ: Vozes, 2007.

MARGAREZI, Andreia Leticia. **Inclusive education and the possibilities of intervention for the social worker.** Brasilia. 2010.

MARTINS, Eliana Bolorino Canteiro. Social Work in Education. **Revista Servigo Social & Realidade**, Franca, v. 8, n. 1, 1999.

MARTINS, Eliana Bolorino Canteiro. Social work in education. **Revista Servipo Social & Realidade**, Franca, v. 18, n. 1, 2009.

MARTINS, Eliana Bolorino Canteiro. Doctoral thesis. **Education and Social Service: a** link for building citizenship. PUC. Sao Paulo 2007.

MAZZOTTA, Marcos J. S. **Educapao especial no Brasil:** historia e politicas publicas. 5. ed. Sao Paulo: Cortez, 2005.

MEC, History. Available at: <http://portal.mec.gov.br/index.php?option=com_content&view=article&id=2& Itemid> Accessed on: August 5, 2011.

REBELO, F. **Contributions of ergonomics to the development of a system to support the professional placement or re-placement of people with disabilities.** In: OMOTE, Sadao. Inclusion: intention and reality. Marilia: 2004

REIS, Marlene Barbosa de Freitas. **Inclusive education:** limits and prospects. Goiania, GO: Deescubra, 2006.

RODRIGUES, Davi. Ten (mis)made ideas about Inclusive Education. In: **Inclusao e educapao:** doze olhares sobre a educapao. inclusive. Sao Paulo: Summus, 2006.

SASSAKI, Romeu K. **Inclusion:** building a society for all. 7. ed. Rio de Janeiro: WVA, 2006.

SAVIANI, Dermeval. **A nova lei da educapao:** trajetorias, limites e perspectivas. ed Autores Associados. Campinas, 1997.

SEGATE, Aline. Teacher Training for School Inclusion of Special Students. In: SEMINARIO DE PESQUISA DO NUPEPE NA UNIVERSIDADE FEDERAL DE UBERLANDIA (UFU), 2, Uberlandia,MG, 2010. **Proceedings...** Uberlandia, MG: UFU, 2010.

SELAU, Bento. **Inclusion in the classroom.** ed. Evangraf. Porto Alegre. 2007.

SIMOES, Ricardo. Historical evolution of the Brazilian electoral system in the constitutions. 2006. Available at <

http://ricardosimoes.com/docs/direito/el_Sistema%20eleitoral%20brasileiro%20-%20evolucao%20historica.pdf> Accessed on: July 2, 2011.

STAINBACK, Susan; STAINBACK, Willan. **Inclusion:** a guide for educators. Porto Alegre: Artes Medicas 1999.

TRIVINOS, A. N. S. **Introdupao a pesquisa em ciencias sociais:** a pesquisa qualitativa em educapao. Sao Paulo: Atlas, 1987.

APENDICES

APPENDIX A - Interview script

I - Profile of Coordinators and Teachers:

- Age/Gender:
- Formapao:

. Course:

. University of training:

. Year completed:

. Time working in education:

. Time working with inclusive education:

. School of acting:

II - Inclusion issues:

1) Have you studied special education? Do you have courses in the area?
2) What disabilities do the students in your school/class have?
3) What is your concept of educational inclusion?
4) Has there been a training course for teachers to work with the inclusion of students with special needs in the ordinary classroom?
5) Can you teach the student with the resources available at school?
6) Do you realize whether inclusion really takes place? What does inclusion contribute to the student's all-round development?
7) What are the negative and positive points of this inclusion policy?
8) What can the social work professional contribute to the implementation of this special education?

MIX
Papier aus verantwortungsvollen Quellen
Paper from responsible sources
FSC® C105338

Printed by Books on Demand GmbH, Norderstedt / Germany